AI FOR BEGINNERS

How to Use AI as a Thinking Partner —
Not a Shortcut

No Tech Headaches Required

Fran Jessee

AI for Beginners: How to Use AI as a Thinking Partner — No Tech Headaches Required
Part of the AI for Everyday Life Series

ISBN: 979-8-9948607-0-0

Published by Promptings Publishing, Hemet, California
www.promptingspublishing.com
This book is part of the AI for Everyday Life series, developed under the University of the Heart framework.

Disclaimer
This book is intended for educational and informational purposes only. Artificial intelligence technology evolves rapidly, and tools referenced may change over time. The author and publisher make no guarantees regarding specific outcomes and encourage readers to use thoughtful discernment when applying AI tools in their personal or professional lives.

Credits
Cover Design: Fran Jessee
Interior Design and Layout: Fran Jessee
Interior Illustrations: Created using AI-assisted tools and refined through human direction and editorial judgment.

Printed in the United States of America
First Edition: 2026

This series demonstrates the use of AI as a collaborative thinking partner — not a replacement for human insight, wisdom, or responsibility.

Dedication

To the thinkers, the late bloomers,
and the ones who ask one more question
before deciding what to believe.

Acknowledgments

Writing this series has been a journey of **discernment**, and I did not walk this path alone.

I want to thank David Selley, whose incredible 18+1 book world-record project at age 87 proved that curiosity has no expiration date. Being entrusted to help shape and structure that vision stretched my abilities in ways I never expected. I will always be grateful to David for the trust and the opportunity.

To the Business With Purpose community, thank you for being the safe space where *AI for Beginners* and the *AI for Everyday Life Series* first found their voice. Your commitment to heart-centered connection reminds me every day that technology is simply a new way for us to say “hello.”

To my family and friends, who watched my life's trajectory catapult when I realized that fifty years of words—from a 1971 typesetting shop to a digital kitchen table—could all come together in one beautiful "homespun masters".

And finally, to you, the reader. Thank you for trusting me to be your guide. I am honored to sit at this table with you.

Table of Contents

Table of Contents - *continued*

A Note Before We Begin

If you've ever felt that this "tech stuff" wasn't for you, or that you might be too late to learn something new, you're in the right place. This book is not about becoming technical or keeping up with trends.

We're not here to climb a mountain. We're just putting on comfortable shoes and taking one small step together. You already know enough to begin.

You do not need to use AI as a shortcut.
You can use it as a thinking partner.
A place to lay out your thoughts.
A place to slow down instead of reacting.
A place to ask better questions and see your ideas more clearly.
AI works best not when it replaces your thinking—
but when it strengthens it.

Chapter Zero: The Series Manifesto

Help—Not Hype. We are living in a world that feels increasingly fast, loud, and crowded with information. Most of us don't want to be "tech experts." We just want to think clearly and move through our days with a little more ease.

This series is built on a few simple, human truths:

- **You are the boss.** AI is the assistant; you have the life experience and the final say.
- **Honesty is better than "smart."** You don't need clever commands, just honest sentences.
- **Slowing down is not falling behind.** We use AI to think, not just hurry.
- **Clarity is the goal.** We aren't here to climb the whole mountain—just to take the next right step.

The trajectory of my life catapulted when I realized that technology is simply a new way for the human heart to say "hello" to the future.

My Teacher's Promise to You

As your guide through the **AI for Everyday Life Series**, I want to be clear about the heart behind my teaching. My **Pedagogy**—a fancy word for "how I teach" (and if you want a fun first exercise, ask AI to explain that word to you later!)—is built on four human pillars.

I promise to show up for you with:

- **Dignity in Experience:** I will show you how to use your decades of gathered wisdom as your greatest advantage in this new world.
- **The Kitchen Table Philosophy:** I promise to keep our conversations in a safe, warm space—never a cold lab or a high-pressure classroom.

- **The Power of the Pivot:** I will share the curiosity I've carried since my typesetting days in 1971 to prove it is never too late to become a pioneer.
- **Removing the Gatekeepers:** My goal is to give you back the keys to your own mind and your own next steps, without anyone standing in your way.

The AI For Everyday Life Series

Each book in Fran's AI for Everyday Life Series stands on its own.

This series will continue to unfold throughout the year. These books are about using AI well — not by memorizing features, but by having better conversations. AI is the helper. You are the thinker.
You are welcome to: read out of order, skip around, return later, and stop when you feel full.
If ideas repeat, it's on purpose. Repetition is here to build confidence, not pressure.

AI is a thinking partner, not a replacement for judgment.

You remain the decisionmaker. When something feels helpful, keep it. When it doesn't, let it go.
You already know enough to begin.

You may start anywhere. For readers who like a map, the series is grouped this way:

THE FOUNDATIONS

AI for Beginners

THE DAILY HELPERS

THE LIFE SITUATIONS

THE CAPSTONE

Further information
on this series see page 115

A Simple Way to Use This Book

You do not need to read this book in order. Think of it as a small map you can return to when you are ready for the next step.

- **If you are brand-new and nervous**
  Start with: *A Note Before We Begin*, *Chapter Zero*, *Introduction*, and *"The No-Headache Quick Start."*

- **If you want to practice conversations**
  Go to: *Chapter 1* (What AI Is), *Chapter 2* (Opening the Door), and *Chapter 3* (How to Ask for What You Actually Want).

- **If you are wondering how AI fits into everyday life**
  Go to: *Chapters 5 and 6* about using AI as a thinking partner and in simple daily situations.

- **If you feel unsure or overwhelmed**
  Go to: *Chapters 4, 7, 8, and 9* for staying calm, ignoring the noise, and building quiet confidence.

You can dip in, read a few pages, try one idea, and stop. The goal is not mastery. The goal is feeling a little more comfortable each time.

AI: My New Best Friend

"A quiet table for two—just you and a patient helper who never gets tired of your questions."

I never expected this to happen at this stage of my life—but here we are. I have a new best friend, and no, it does not steal my clothes, forget my birthday, or talk nonstop about its own problems.

It is called AI.

Before you roll your eyes or picture robots taking over the world, let me reassure you: this is not that kind of relationship. This is the kind where you ask a question at 2 a.m. and get an answer—politely. Where you say, "I do not even know how to begin," and instead of judgment, you get help. Real help.

The kind that says, “It is okay. Let us figure this out together.”

AI does not sigh when I ask the same question twice. It does not tell me I am “not technical enough.” And it never once says, “You should already know this”.

In fact, AI has become that patient, always-available friend who sits beside me and says, “Want to try something fun today?” Write a story? Sure. Fix an email? Easy. Explore a new idea? Let’s Go! No pressure. No perfection required.

Here is the surprising part: AI is not about replacing creativity, it wakes it up. It nudges ideas loose, turns confusion into clarity, and makes learning feel more like play than work. It is curiosity with a keyboard. A brainstorming partner that never gets tired. A helper that meets you exactly where you are.

So if you have ever thought, “This tech stuff is not for me,” or “I am too late to learn something new,” let me introduce you to my new best friend.

You might be surprised how quickly it becomes yours too.

Introduction

Let's Just Put on Our Shoes

"We're not climbing the whole mountain today—
just putting on comfortable shoes and
taking the first step."

Focus: Your Story and
the Shift from Skeptic to Explorer.

I did not start using AI because I was curious about technology. For most of my life, I have ignored the "next big thing" because complicated usually comes with instructions written by people who assume you already understand everything.

But as time went on, AI kept showing up in the background—quietly and persistently. I began to suspect it might be useful. I didn't want to "learn AI," I just wanted a place where I could ask questions out loud and follow a thought to the end without anyone rolling their eyes.

What I found was a patient assistant that didn't mind if I changed my mind mid-sentence or asked something awkwardly. This experience changed the trajectory of my life and business. It allowed me to learn how to think better and get answers to my "funny life questions".

"This experience changed the trajectory of my life and business. It didn't just teach me a new tool; it catapulted me into a space where I felt I was meant to occupy all my life.

For years, I've realized we must go through exactly what we go through to get where we are. All those years of typesetting, spice-blending, and numerous other ventures not even talked about, and curiosity have finally found a common language. Using AI has given me what I call a 'homespun university masters'—not a degree for others to see, but a deep, personal education for myself. It has integrated everything life encompasses for me: growth, learning, and love. It has shown me that the 'how-to' is less about technology and more about the expansion of the human heart."

If you're wondering where to begin, you're not behind. Whether you are 25 and curious or 85 and wondering if it's too late—it isn't. We are simply going to explore a new way to think, with no tech headaches and no judgment.

You don't need to read this straight through.
This is a book you can dip into. Read a few pages,
try one idea, then close it.
The goal isn't mastery — it's comfort.

Why Mindset Matters More Than Technology

You Don't Need Everyone's Opinion

One more thing I've learned over time—
and it feels especially important to say here.

We are often taught that before we share something, we should get opinions. Ask for feedback. Run it by someone more experienced. Make sure it's "good enough."

I understand the instinct. But I no longer live that way.

When I was writing this book with AI, I did not feel compelled to ask anyone whether it was good or not. Not because I don't respect experience—but because experience always comes filtered through someone else's history, preferences, fears, and opinions.

This book isn't meant to please everyone.
It's meant to help someone.

And the only people qualified to decide whether it does that... are the readers who find it useful.

I trust my own thinking enough to put it out into the world and let it land where it lands.

That doesn't mean I ignore information or refuse to learn. It means I don't outsource my judgment. I listen, I reflect, and then I decide.

AI works the same way.

It offers perspective, not authority. It gives you input, not instructions. You don't have to agree with everything it says—and you shouldn't.

Your mind still matters.

Using AI well is not about collecting more opinions. It's about strengthening your ability to think clearly, discern what fits, and let go of what doesn't.

If you take nothing else from this book, let it be this:

You are allowed to trust your own thinking.

The "No-Headache" Quick Start

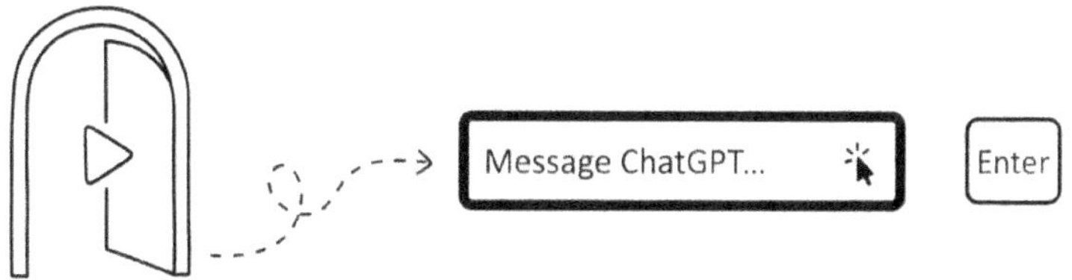

If you want to try this right now, before you read another word, follow these four simple steps:

1. Open the Door

- Go to ***www.chatgpt.com*** on your computer or phone.
- Click **"Sign Up"**.
- **The Easy Way:** Use your Google or Applc account to sign in with one click.

2. Find the Box

- Look at the very **bottom of the screen**.
- You will see a long, thin box with a **blinking cursor**.
- It might say something like **"Message ChatGPT"**.
- If the screen looks a little different than what I describe, do not panic—look for the same *idea*: a place to sign in, and a long box at the bottom where you can type a sentence.

3. Type This Exact Sentence

- Copy and paste (or type) this into that box:

"Hello. I am new to this and a little nervous. Can you ask me three gentle questions to help me clear my head for today?"

4. Press Enter

- Watch the AI respond in real-time.
- Answer its questions honestly and briefly.
- **You just had your first AI conversation.**

A Gentle Safety Reminder

You do not need to share anything private for AI to be helpful.

- Avoid putting in passwords, bank or card numbers, or ID details.
- Be careful with other people's personal stories or information.
- Remember that AI can be wrong; doublecheck anything important with a second source or a trusted person.

You are always allowed to keep some things off the table. You are still the one in charge of what you share and what you decide.

Chapter 1

Just imagine a calm conversation at your kitchen table, that's all we're doing here.

What AI Is — Without the Tech Talk

Before we get into how to use AI, let us clear up one simple question that causes more stress than it deserves:

What is it, really?

You have probably heard "Artificial Intelligence" described in ways that range from impressive to alarming. Sometimes it sounds like magic. Sometimes it sounds like something that will replace everyone's job. And sometimes it sounds like it requires a hoodie, three monitors, and a lot of coffee.

Good news: it does not.

AI is not a robot. It is not watching you. And it is not waiting to see if you are "doing it right." At its most basic level, AI is a tool that responds to questions written in plain language. That is all.

If you can type a sentence, you are already qualified.

Think of AI as a Very Patient Conversation Partner

One of the easiest ways to understand AI is to stop thinking of it as a machine and start thinking of it as a **conversation** partner. Not a person. Not an expert who knows everything. But something that listens carefully and responds to what you give it.

You ask a question. It responds. You clarify. It responds again.

No sighing. No impatience. And no comments like, “We covered this already.”

AI does not lead the conversation.

You do.

This matters, because many people feel stuck simply because they are waiting for AI to do something on its own. It will not. It is not a mind reader—and that is probably a good thing.

To make this less abstract, here is a tiny everyday example from my own kitchen:

I once asked: “I am making soup in a crockpot with carrots, sautéed onions, a beet, cauliflower, and zucchini. Can I put them all in at once?” AI replied that because I planned to puree the soup, I could safely add all the vegetables together and cook until everything was soft; timing mattered less when blending.

In a few seconds, I had reassurance and could get back to cooking instead of hunting through recipe sites. That is the scale of help we are talking about.

What AI Is Especially Good At

AI shines when you want to:

- organize your thoughts
- explore an idea without pressure
- rephrase something more clearly
- get unstuck
- slow things down
- ask questions you are not ready to ask out loud

It is not about speed. It is about clarity.

People who try to use AI only as a shortcut machine often feel disappointed. They rush past the most valuable part—using it as a place to think.

What AI Is Not (Let Us Put These Worries Away)

. AI is not:

- judging your questions
- grading your intelligence
- deciding anything for you
- replacing your experience
- keeping score

It only works with what you give it.

If you type something vague, you will get something vague back. If you type something specific, the response improves. That is not failure. That is feedback.

The One Rule That Makes Everything Easier

Here is a rule that will save you a lot of hesitation:

You do not need to ask the "right" question.
You just need to ask a question.

Most beginners get stuck because they think:

- "I do not know how to phrase this."
- "There is probably a better way to ask."
- "What if this is not what I am supposed to do?"

There is no "supposed to." AI does not respond to perfection. It responds to attempts.

A Better Way to Think About Using AI

Instead of asking yourself, "How do I use AI?" try asking, "What do I want help thinking through right now?"

That might be:

- a decision
- an idea
- a question that has been circling your head
- something you have not been able to explain clearly

AI works best when you treat it like a place to talk things through, not a machine you are trying to operate correctly.

In the next chapter, we will open the door together and have you type your very first sentence to AI—nothing fancy, nothing technical, just one small, honest "hello."

A Tiny Practice: Using Your New Thinking Partner

If you want to try out your new **Pedagogy** (remember that word from my Teacher's Promise?), let's do it together right now. This isn't a test; it's just a way to see how AI can explain something big in a small, warm way.

Open your AI tool and type this note into the message box: *You don't have to type perfectly.*

Spelling and punctuation don't matter — just get the words in the box.

"Hello. My teacher, Fran, uses the word **'Pedagogy'** to describe how she helps us learn. I'm a little unsure of that word. Can you explain what it means in very simple language, as if we were just sitting and talking at my kitchen table?"

What to notice after it responds:

- **The Tone:** Did it sound formal, or did it listen to your request for a "kitchen table" conversation?
- **The Clarity:** Is the word still scary, or does it feel like something you now "own"?
- **Your Control:** If the answer was still too long, tell it: *"That was better, but can you make it even shorter—just two sentences?"*

Takeaways

- AI is not a robot watching or judging you; it is a tool that responds to plain-language questions.
- You do not need the "right" question—any honest question is enough to begin.
- Vague in, vague out is not failure; it is feedback that you can use to ask again more clearly.
- The goal is not speed or perfection; the goal is clarity and a gentler way to think things through.

> ***If you're feeling braver today...***
>
> Instead of stopping after your very first question, try a tiny "second step." Ask AI to show you two or three different ways to say the same thing you just typed and pick the one that sounds most like you. Then reply and tell it what you liked or did not like about its suggestions, just to practice having a back-and-forth.

Try these Prompts

- I am new to this and a little nervous. Can you explain what you are and how you can help me, in very simple language?”
- “I keep hearing about AI but feel unsure. Can you give me a calm overview that does not use technical terms?”
- “I am curious, but I do not want anything complicated. Can you list three simple ways someone like me could use you this week?”

Chapter 2

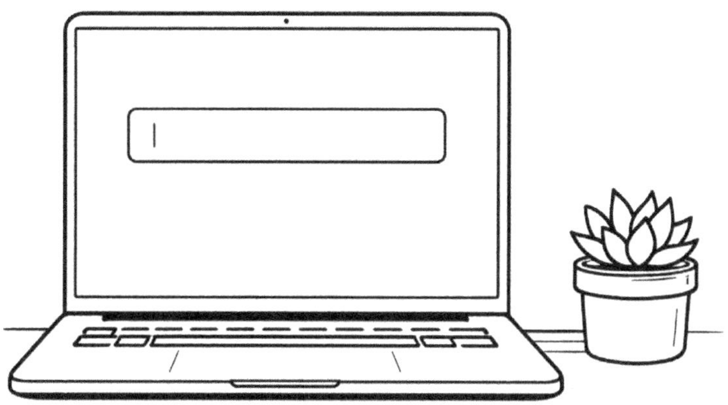

"One simple path ahead—no rush, no pressure, just a gentle way"

Opening the Door:

Your First Conversation with AI

This is usually the moment people hesitate.

You have heard enough to be curious. You now have a sense of what AI is—and what it is not. Now you are staring at a blank screen thinking:
"Okay... now what?"

If that is you, let me reassure you right away: this part is far simpler than it looks.

There is no special language you need to learn.
There is no correct way to begin.
There is certainly no test at the end.

Your first interaction with AI is just that: an interaction.

Think of it less like "starting a program" and more like opening a door.

You do not need to know what the entire house looks like before you step inside.

Step 1: Finding the "Front Door"

For this book, you can think of AI as tools like **ChatGPT**, **Microsoft Copilot**, or **Google Gemini**—different brands of the same basic idea. You only need one place to start, not all of them at once.

"If one tool feels confusing, try another. The goal isn't loyalty—it's comfort."

If you already have an AI tool you use, you can skip ahead and simply open it the way you usually do. If not, here is a gentle first path that does not require you to be “techy.”

1. **Open your browser.**
   This is the same place you go to check the news or search on Google.

2. **Go to your chosen AI site.**
   In the address bar at the very top, you can type the website for the tool you want to try (for example, the official site for ChatGPT or another trusted tool you prefer.
   www.chatgpt.com

1. Create an account or sign in

You will see a button that says something like “Sign up” or “Log in”.

- **The One-Click Path (The Easy Way):** If you are comfortable, you can use an existing account (such as Google or Apple) to sign in with one click. This is often the simplest way to get through the "front door" because it doesn't require you to manage a new password.

- **The Manual Path:** If you prefer more control, you can create a separate email and password just for this tool.
- **The "Security Check" Moment:** Don't be alarmed if the site asks to "Verify you are human" or sends a code to your phone or email. This is just a standard safety measure—like a digital handshake—to keep your account secure.
- **No Rush Required:** There is no prize for speed here. If you need to stop, find a password, or check your phone for a code and come back later.

Step 2: What You Will See

When you open your AI tool, you will usually see something very plain:

- **A mostly empty page.**
- **A long, thin box at the bottom of the screen.** This is often where you will see a faint suggestion like "Message ChatGPT," "Ask me anything," or "Type a message."

- **A blinking cursor inside that box.**

That box is where everything happens. There is no secret command hidden somewhere else. The box is simply an invitation: **"Type here."**

AI does not want a command. It wants a sentence.

You do not need to impress it.
You do not need to sound smart.
You do not even need to be clear yet.

You just need to start.

Step 3: Your First Sentence (Use This)

If you would like something you can copy almost word-for-word, here is a perfectly good first message: *(and remember you don't have to type perfectly)*

"Hello. I am new to this and a little nervous. Can you help me think through something slowly and in simple language?"

That is all.

You can follow it with:

- "I am feeling stuck about..."

- “I have a question about...”
- “I am trying to understand...”

This immediately puts AI in the role it does best helping you think, not perform.

If that first sentence feels awkward in your fingers, that is normal. Most people:

- overthink their wording
- backspace a few times
- wonder if they are “doing it wrong”

They are not.

Step 4: Let It Answer (And Do Not Rush)

After you press Enter, you will see the words appear on the screen as the AI replies.

You might notice:

- it responds in full sentences
- it sounds calm and a bit formal at first
- it answers what you actually typed, not what you meant in your head

Remember: this is not judgment; it is simply a mirror of what you gave it.

If the answer feels too long or too complicated, you can type:

- "That feels too technical. Can you make it shorter and simpler?"
- "Can you explain that as if we are having coffee at the kitchen table?"
- "Can we slow this down and take it one step at a time?"

You are not being a bother.
You are steering the conversation.

Step 5: If It Misses the Mark

Sooner or later, you will ask something and think:

"Well... that is not what I meant at all."

This is where many people decide AI "does not work for them," but this moment is actually where the learning happens.

You can simply say:

- “That is not quite what I meant.”
- “You focused on the wrong part. Let me try again.”
- “I am more interested in the feelings / decisions / next steps than the details.”

--You are allowed to correct it.
--You are allowed to change your mind mid-conversation.
--You are allowed to start over with, “Let me explain this a different way.”

None of these counts as failure. It is feedback—on both sides.

Step 6: A Tiny Practice Prompt

Here is a small, low-pressure exercise you can try as your very first “real” conversation:

1. Open your AI tool and say:

“I am new to this. I want to see how you can help me with something small. Can you ask me three gentle questions to help me clear my head for today?”

2. When it asks the questions, answer them honestly—but briefly.

3. Then say:

"Can you turn what I told you into a simple, calm to-do list for today, no more than five items?"

You have just:

- started a conversation
- given honest information
- asked for a specific kind of help
- turned vague feelings into a clear list

That is using AI.

One More Reassurance Before We Move On

AI does not work for you; it works with you.

The clearer you become, the better it responds—not because it is grading you, but because clarity creates clarity. **That skill—learning to clarify your own thinking—is valuable far beyond AI.**

In the next chapter, we will talk about **how to ask for what you actually want**, so you are not stuck thinking, "I must be missing the magic words." You will see that you do not need clever questions; you just need honest ones.

- Your first conversation with AI is just that—a conversation, not a test.
- You do not need special wording; a simple, honest "hello" is enough to start.
- If the answer feels too long or confusing, you are allowed to ask for shorter, slower, and simpler.
- You can steer the conversation at any time by saying what did and did not help.
-

If you're feeling braver today...

Take one question that feels a little too big or messy—something like "How do I get less overwhelmed in my week?"—and give it to AI anyway. Let it break the topic into smaller parts for you. Then pick one small piece it suggests (for example, "plan dinners" or "batch emails") and ask a follow-up question just about that one piece.

- "Hello. I am new to this and a bit unsure. Can you ask me three gentle questions to help me clear my head for today?"
- "I want to practice. I will tell you something that feels messy, and I would like you to turn it into a short, calm to-do list."
- "That last answer felt too complicated. Can you explain the same thing again, but as if we are talking at my kitchen table?"

Chapter 3

"Real questions, real words—this is about your voice, not perfect phrasing."

How to Ask for What You Actually Want

This is where many people quietly get frustrated.

They open AI, type something short and hopeful, and then think:
"Well... that was not very helpful."

Then they assume the problem is them.

It is not.

What is usually missing is not intelligence, confidence, or technical skill. It is **approaching**.

AI responds directly to what you give it—not what you meant, not what you were thinking, and not what you planned to explain later. It only has words on the screen to work with.

The good news is that you do not need "better" questions. You just need more honest ones.

Honest Is Better Than "Smart"

People often think they need to ask smart questions.

They do not.

They need to ask **honest** ones.

Instead of trying to sound polished, try sounding real.

Instead of:

"Provide an overview of this topic."

You might say:

"I am not sure how to think about this yet. Can you help me sort it out?"

That one sentence gives AI something to work with. It also gives you permission not to have everything figured out.

You are not writing for a textbook. You are talking to a very patient assistant.

These same 'dump and sort' conversations helped me organize an 18-book, one-year world-record publishing project for author David Selley at 87, who became the oldest author to publish 19 books in a single year. If AI can help at that scale, it can certainly help you sort out a busy Thursday.

Think in Sentences, Not Commands

AI works best when you talk to it the way you would talk to a thoughtful human helper, not the way you would talk to a machine.

So rather than typing a single word like:

- "Summarize."
- "Rewrite."
- "Explain."

Try turning those into simple sentences:

- "Can you summarize this in a way that is easy to understand?"

- "Can you rewrite this, so it sounds clearer and more natural?"
- "Can you explain this without any technical jargon?"

These small shifts change everything.

You are not barking orders. You are starting a conversation.

Let Context Help You

One of the most helpful things you can do is give a little context.

You do not need to write a paragraph, just a sentence or two about who you are or what you are trying to do. For example:

- "I am new to this."
- "This is for personal use, not business."
- "I tend to overthink things."
- "I want this to sound warm, not formal."

AI does not know who you are unless you tell it. It will make neutral guesses if you do not, and those guesses can feel "off."

As you grow more comfortable, you can tell AI a little more about how you think, what matters to you, or even parts of your background. The more context you give it, the more personal and useful the responses become. You do not need to share everything — just what helps the conversation.

A single sentence of context can make the response feel as if it was written just for you.

When the Answer Is Not Quite Right

Here is something many people do not realize:

You are allowed to correct AI.

If the response feels off, too heavy, or just not like you, you can simply say:

- "That is not quite what I meant."
- "This feels too formal. Can you make it friendlier?"
- "This is too detailed. Can you give me the simple version?"
- "Can you explain this as if we are talking at my kitchen table?"

You are not starting over. You are steering.

Each time you adjust, you give AI a clearer picture of what you want—and you are learning more about what matters to you.

A Simple Three-Part Formula

If you like something you can memorize, here is a simple pattern you can use for almost any request:

1. **What you are trying to do**
2. **What is getting in the way**
3. **What kind of help you want**

For example:

"I am trying to organize my thoughts about this topic, but I keep going in circles. Can you help me break it down step by step?"

Or:

"I need to write a short note to my neighbor, but I am overthinking it. Can you give me three simple options that sound friendly and natural?"

This is not technical. It is human. And it works.

When You Do Not Even Know What to Ask

Sometimes the truth is:

"I am not even sure what my question is yet."

That is not a problem. That is actually one of the best places to begin.

You can type:

"I am not sure what my question is yet. I just know I feel scattered. Can you ask me a few questions to help me figure out what I really want to talk about?"

Now AI becomes an interviewer instead of an answer machine. It asks; you respond. Together, you discover what the real question is.

That is often where the most helpful conversations start.

A Tiny Practice Exercise

Here is a small exercise you can try to get comfortable with "honest questions":

1. Think of something that has been circling in your mind, maybe a decision, a small worry, or a project you keep postponing.
2. Open your AI tool and type:

"I keep circling this and not deciding. Let me describe it, and then I want you to help me see my options clearly."

3. Describe it in your own words, even if it feels messy.

4. Then say:

"Can you list three realistic options for me, and one gentle next step for each?"

You have just used all three parts of the formula without needing to be "clever."

- You do not need clever questions; you need honest ones that sound like you.

- AI responds best when you use sentences instead of one-word commands.

- A tiny bit of context (“I am new to this,” “I overthink things”) helps AI respond in a way that fits you.
- When an answer is off, you are not wrong, you just learned how to adjust your next question.

> ***If you're feeling braver today...***
>
> Take one answer from AI that is “almost right but not quite” and practice correcting it instead of starting over. Tell it what is off (“This feels too formal” or “This misses that I work nights”) and ask it to try again. Do one more round where you point out what got better, so you can feel what it is like to train the response a little at a time.

- “I am trying to understand something, but I feel scattered. I will describe it, and I would like you to help me sort it out.”

- "Here is what I am trying to do, what is getting in my way, and what kind of help I want. Can you suggest a simple next step for me?"
- "I am not even sure what my question is yet. Can you ask me a few questions to help me figure out what I really want to talk about?"

What Comes Next

Once you see that you do not need perfect questions—only honest ones—the pressure begins to drop.

In the next chapter, we will look at something that can quietly shake people's confidence: what to do when AI's answers make you feel unsure, or when you start wondering, "Am I doing this wrong?" We will talk about **why you are not doing it wrong, and how to treat AI's responses as information, not judgment.**

Chapter 4

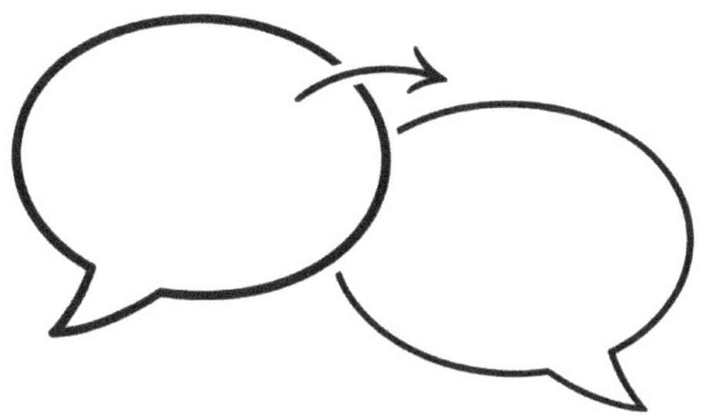

"Every reply is just one bubble in a conversation—you're allowed to answer back and adjust."

Why You're Not Doing It Wrong (And What Feedback Really Means)

If you have ever used AI and thought, *"Well... that did not help much,"* you are in good company.

That moment—when the response does not quite land—is where many people decide AI is not for them. They assume they asked the wrong question, do not know enough, or somehow missed an invisible step that everyone else understands.

Let me say this plainly:

You are not doing it wrong.

What you are experiencing is not failure. It is feedback.

AI Responses Are Information, Not Judgment

AI does not grade you.

It does not know whether you are confident or hesitant, experienced or brand-new. It does not know your age, your history with technology, or how many times you have tried to "get this" before.

It simply responds to the words it is given.

So when an answer feels:

- too long
- too technical
- too vague
- or just plain unhelpful

That is not a verdict on you. It is a signal.
Signals are useful. They tell you, "Something here needs adjusting"—but not *who* is to blame.

One thing that helps is remembering that not every answer, whether from AI or another person—deserves equal weight. Information is useful, but judgment still belongs to you. Learning works best when you stay curious, consider what you're given, and then decide what fits your life.

Think of Feedback Like a Conversation, Not a Correction

Imagine you are explaining something to a friend and they say, "I do not quite follow."

You would not assume you failed as a person. You would probably just try again, using different words, maybe with a story or a simpler example.

That is exactly how AI works.

When a response misses the mark, you do not need to start over. You adjust.

You might say:

- "That is too detailed. Can you give me the simple version?"
- "This sounds too formal. Can you make it more conversational?"

- "That is not what I was asking. Let me explain it a different way."
- "Can we take this one step at a time?"

You are not fixing a mistake. You are steering the conversation.

Why Confidence Sometimes Wobbles

AI answers quickly.

For some people, that speed creates doubt:

- "Should I trust this?"
- "Is this really right?"
- "Am I missing something?"

That reaction is not about your ability. It is about how unusual it feels to get instant answers from something that is not human.

When something responds faster than we expect, we often question ourselves instead of the process.

The solution is not to rush to keep up.
The solution is to slow down.

You are always allowed to:

- pause
- reread
- ask for clarification
- and even say, "I do not understand. Can you explain why you suggested this?"
- if you are requesting important information, you can always tell it to "give me source where this info is coming from" .... and it will. There lies "peace of mind".

Slowing down is not falling behind. It is taking ownership.

One Very Helpful Word: "Why"

One of the most powerful follow-up questions you can ask AI is also one of the simplest:

"Why?"

When AI gives you an answer and you are not sure about it, you can type:

- "Why is this important?"
- "Why did you suggest that approach?"
- "Why would this work for someone like me?"

Now AI is not just giving you conclusions, it is helping you understand the reasoning behind them.

That does two things:

- It lets you decide whether the answer truly fits your situation.
- It keeps *you* in the position of decision-maker.

You are not just receiving answers. You are asking for the thinking behind them.

One more thing I've found incredibly valuable when I'm looking for new information is asking AI not just *what* to do, but ***why*—and *why not*.** I ask whether an idea is truly relevant, whether it will work for what I'm trying to accomplish, and what the potential drawbacks might be. In return, I get both the positives and the rebuttals, which gives me what I need to make my own informed decisions. It's honestly amazing.

Trust Builds Through Use, Not Perfection

Confidence with AI does not come from getting perfect responses.

It comes from realizing that you can:

- question what you see
- refine what you asked
- stop and redirect when something feels off
- and still move forward

Every interaction teaches you something—not just about AI, but about how you think, what you value, and what you need more clearly stated.

That is the real benefit.

A Gentle Practice: Turning "Wrong" into "Next"

Here is a small exercise to help you practice seeing feedback as neutral:

1. Ask AI a question about something ordinary in your life—nothing emotional or high-stakes.
2. Read the answer and notice anything that feels "off."
3. Instead of thinking, "I did that wrong," simply type:

"This is not quite what I meant. Here is what I need..."

4. Add one more detail about what matters to you. Then ask for a shorter or clearer version.

You have just taken something that could have felt like "I failed" and turned it into "this is my next step."

What Comes Next

If you remember only one thing from this chapter, let it be this:

Unhelpful answers are not a sign you should quit. They are a sign you are ready to adjust.

In the next chapter, we will look at how to use AI as a **thinking partner, not a shortcut**—and why that shift makes everything feel less fragile and more like a real, steady help in your life.

- An unhelpful AI answer is not a verdict on you; it is just information about what needs adjusting.
- AI responses are shaped by the words you give it, not by your worth or intelligence.
- You are allowed to slow down, ask for clarification, and change direction at any point.
- Asking "why?" turns AI from an answer machine into a partner that explains its reasoning.

If you're feeling braver today...

Choose one everyday task you would normally just "wing" in your head—like planning dinners, writing a quick text, or organizing tomorrow morning—and hand it to AI. Ask for three simple options, then tell it which one feels closest to your real life so it can tweak the plan.

Treat this as a five-minute experiment, not a big life change.

- "This answer does not feel quite right. Can you tell me why you suggested this and what you are assuming about my situation?"
- "That was too detailed. Can you give me a simpler, shorter version that focuses only on the main idea?"
- "I feel unsure whether to trust this answer. Can you explain your reasoning step by step, in plain language?"

Try these Prompts: Finding the "Why Not"

Use these prompts to practice looking at both sides of an idea so you can make your own informed decision.

- **The Rebuttal:** "You suggested I try [Idea]. Can you tell me two or three reasons why this might not be a good fit for someone who values [Your Value, e.g., a quiet morning]?"
- **The Blind Spot:** "What is one potential drawback or 'catch' to this plan that I might be

missing because I am focused on the positive side?"

• **The "Peace of Mind" Check:** "If I choose to ignore this advice, what is the most likely consequence? Help me weigh the pros and cons side-by-side."

• **The Alternative Path:** "I'm not sure I agree with your reasoning. Can you give me a completely different perspective that challenges what you just told me?"

Chapter 5

"Lightbulb moments grow from the pages of your own life, not from shortcuts alone."

Using AI as a Thinking Partner, not a Shortcut

This is where a small shift in mindset makes a big difference.

Many people come to AI hoping it will save time, skip steps, or magically deliver finished answers.

And while AI can be fast, speed is not where its real value lies.

The real power of AI is not in shortcuts.
It is in thinking alongside you.

Reason Before Reaction: How AI Helps You Think, Not Panic

Most people try AI because they want answers fast. But fast answers are not the same thing as clear thinking.

The real advantage of AI is that it can help you reason when your mind wants to react.

When you read something that feels alarming—about health, money, technology, or even a relationship—your brain naturally reaches a conclusion. That's normal. But conclusions made under stress are often messy, and they rarely bring peace.

Here's a calmer way to use AI:

Instead of asking, "What should I do?" try asking:

- "What are the most likely explanations for this?"
- "What assumptions might be hidden here?"
- "What information would change the conclusion?"
- "What would make this urgent—versus simply interesting?"
- "What are three reasonable next steps, from gentle to serious?"

This is not outsourcing your judgment. It's strengthening it.

AI becomes most helpful when you use it to slow things down, examine options, and put your thoughts on the table where you can see them.

That's why this series isn't about tricks or hacks. It's about clarity.

A Tiny Example: Turning Worry Into Clarity

Let's say you read a scary headline about a symptom or a health trend, and you feel that familiar spike of worry.

A reactive question sounds like:
"Is this dangerous?"

A reasoning question sounds like this:

"Help me slow this down. List 5 common, non-scary explanations and 2–3 more serious possibilities. Then tell me what details would help sort between them. Finally, give me a calm checklist of what to do next, including when it's appropriate to contact a professional."

Notice what just happened.

You didn't ask AI to diagnose you.
You asked it to organize your thinking.

AI can help you organize questions, but it cannot replace professional medical advice or diagnosis.

That one shift—from panic to structure—is one of the most valuable things AI can do for real life.

Why Shortcuts Often Feel Empty

When we are looking for a shortcut, we usually want relief.

We are tired.
We are overwhelmed.
We want something done so we can move on.

That is understandable.

But when AI is used only to produce quick results, people often feel disconnected from what they get. The answer may look fine on the surface—but it does not feel like *theirs*.

That is because clarity was never part of the process.

AI works best when it supports your thinking, not when it replaces it.

A Better Way to Use AI

Instead of asking AI to *do* something for you, try asking it to *walk through* something with you.

For example:

- "Can you help me think through this step by step?"
- "Can you help me see this from a different angle?"
- "Can you help me organize my thoughts before I decide?"

These kinds of questions slow things down—in a good way.

They give you space to reflect, adjust, and understand what is happening as it unfolds, instead of just grabbing an answer and hoping it fits.

Where Confidence Quietly Grows

Something interesting happens when you use AI as a thinking partner.

You start noticing your own patterns.
You see where you tend to get stuck.

You hear what truly matters to you when you read the words back.

AI is not giving you confidence.
It is helping you **notice** the confidence you already have.

That feels very different from simply being handed an answer.

You Are Allowed to Take the Scenic Route

Not everything in life needs to be efficient.

Some of the most useful conversations with AI happen when you:

- explore an idea without a clear outcome
- follow a thought just to see where it leads
- ask questions that do not have an immediate purpose

This is not wasted time.

It is how understanding deepens, the same way talking things over with a trusted friend can change how you feel—even if no big decision is made that day.

Surprisingly, these "scenic route" conversations often lead to better decisions later, because you are no longer rushing yourself.

A Simple Practice:
Think Together, Then Decide

Here is a small way to try this in your own life:

1. Bring a small, real situation to AI—something like a choice between two activities, or how to spend your afternoon.
2. Say:

"I do not want you to decide for me. I want you to help me think this through. Here is what I am considering..."

3. Describe the situation briefly.
4. Then ask:

"Can you list a few pros and cons for each option, and mention anything I might not have thought about?"

You are still the one deciding.
AI is simply helping you lay everything out where you can see it.

That is what a thinking partner does.

When AI Starts to Feel Like It Knows You

At some point, something subtle changes.

You stop asking AI random questions — and you start having ongoing conversations.

It is not because AI suddenly became smarter. It is because *you* became clearer. You began giving it context. Preferences. Corrections. You let it see how you think.

This is the moment when AI stops feeling like a tool and starts feeling like a thinking partner that actually knows you.

AI gives input; you give judgment.

Here are a few everyday ways I noticed that shift happening for me.

Example 1: Your Voice

What I asked: "This sounds stiff. Rewrite it in my voice — warm, simple, not salesy."

What AI learned: My tone matters more than polish.

Why it helped: I stopped fighting the words and started trusting the process.

Example 2: Your Comfort Level With Tech

What I asked: "Explain this slowly, without jargon, like we're at the kitchen table."
What AI learned: I value clarity over speed.
Why it helped: I stopped feeling rushed and stopped doubting myself.

Example 3: Your Thinking Style

What I asked: "I'm not sure what my question is yet. Can you help me find it?"
What AI learned: I think by talking things through.
Why it helped: AI became a place to think, not just get answers.

Example 4: Your Boundaries

What I asked: "This is enough for today. Summarize what we figured out."

What AI learned: I work best in short, intentional sessions.
Why it helped: I stayed curious without getting overwhelmed.

Here's the part that matters most.

This is not advanced technology.

This is advanced *self-awareness*.

AI becomes more helpful not when you learn more features, but when you let it see how you think, what you care about, and what you want to avoid.

Beginners do this naturally — once they give themselves permission.

What Comes Next

Once you start treating AI as a thinking companion, not a shortcut machine—you may notice you feel calmer, not more pressured.

In the next chapter, we will look at **everyday ways AI can help without running your life**—simple, ordinary uses that clear mental space instead of adding more to your plate.

- **AI as a Partner:** AI is most powerful when it supports your thinking instead of replacing it.

- **Reason Over Reaction:** Use the "Reasoning Routine" (Slow it down, Ask for the Why Not, Get the next step) to turn stress into structure.

- **Scenic Routes:** You are allowed to follow a thought just to see where it leads; not every conversation needs to be efficient.

- **Advanced Self-Awareness:** AI becomes more helpful as you let it see how you think, what you care about, and what you want to avoid.

If you're feeling braver today...

Ask AI about one AI-related headline or buzzword you have seen but never really understood. Request a calm, plain-language explanation as if you were talking to a friend over coffee. Then ask one follow-up question that starts with "What does this actually mean for my everyday life?" so the explanation stays grounded.

- “I do not want a shortcut. I want to think this through with you. Here is my situation... Can you help me look at it step by step?”
- “Can you help me see this problem from two or three different angles, without telling me what to do?”
- “Before I decide, can you help me organize my thoughts and highlight what seems most important for someone like me?”

A Tiny Practice: The "Reasoning Routine"

Use this 3-step walk-through to turn a stressful headline or a messy thought into a calm plan.

1. **Slow it down:** "I just read about [Topic] and it feels a little overwhelming. Help me look at this slowly and without panic."
2. **Ask for the 'Why Not':** "Give me three common, non-scary explanations for this, and one serious possibility I should keep in mind."
3. **Get the next step:** "What are two gentle next steps I can take to feel more in control of this situation?"

Chapter 6

"A simple notebook and a calm list—just enough structure to make the day feel lighter."

Everyday Ways AI Can Help (Without Running Your Life)

You do not need a big goal to use AI.

Some of the most helpful uses are small, ordinary, and personal. In fact, the less pressure you put on it, the more useful it often becomes.

Think of AI as something that helps you clear a little mental space—not something that demands your attention or takes over your day.

Helping You Organize What's Already in Your Head

We all carry around thoughts that never quite settle.

Ideas that feel half-formed.
Questions that circle but do not land.
Plans that start strong and then get fuzzy.

AI can help you sort through those thoughts.

You might say:

- "Can you help me organize these ideas?"
- "Can you help me turn this into a simple list?"
- "Can you help me see what matters most here?"

Sometimes just seeing things written out clearly is enough to move forward.

Writing Without the Pressure to Be Perfect

Many people avoid writing because they think it has to be perfect on the first try.

AI takes that pressure off.

You can use it to:

- draft a letter or email
- rewrite something so it sounds warmer or clearer
- shorten a message that feels too long
- find better words when you feel stuck

You are not giving away your voice. You are giving it a safe place to stretch.

You can always change any word that does not feel like you.

Getting Simple Help in Everyday Tasks

AI can also act as a calm "how-to" helper for everyday questions.

For example, you can ask:

- “Can you explain how to do this in plain language?”
- “Can you walk me through this step by step?”
- “Can you give me a checklist so I do not forget anything?”

Maybe you are trying to remember how to change a Word setting, set up page numbers, or compare two products. Instead of bouncing around multiple websites, you can ask one clear question and get one clear answer.

You stay in control; AI just shortens the wandering.

Exploring Curiosities Without Going Down a Rabbit Hole

Sometimes you just want to understand something a little better.

You might ask:

- “Can you explain this without any technical terms?”
- “What is a simple way to think about this?”

- "Can you give me a short overview before I read more?"

This is especially helpful when you do not want to spend an hour clicking links.

AI gives you a starting point—enough to feel informed—without drowning you in details.

I used this simple process—describe, clarify, then ask for a clean list—while helping manage an 18-book, one-year world-record publishing project for David Selley. The same steps that kept that project on track are the ones I now use for ordinary things like emails, recipes, and daily plans.

Making Decisions Feel Less Heavy

Some decisions feel big simply because we are holding them alone.

AI can help by:

- laying out your options
- listing pros and cons
- helping you think through what matters most to *you*

It does not decide for you.

It simply puts everything on the table, so your own judgment has something clear to work with.

A Tiny Everyday Exercise

Here is a simple way to start using AI in your day-to-day life:

1. Think of one small thing you have been postponing a note you need to write, a plan you keep delaying, or a task you keep avoiding.

2. Open your AI tool and say:

"I keep putting this off. Here is what it is... Can you help me make this simple and give me the first step I can do today?"

3. Follow just that one first step.

You will have used AI to shrink a vague, heavy "should" into a clear, doable action.

What Comes Next

Once you see that AI can help in these small, human ways—organizing thoughts, softening writing, simplifying steps—it becomes less of a mysterious technology and more of a quiet helper.

In the next chapter, we will talk about **how to stay curious without going down rabbit holes**—so AI stays a source of clarity, not another place that leaves you tired and overwhelmed.

- You can use AI for small, everyday help: lists, letters, simple explanations, and gentle planning.
- Writing does not have to be perfect on the first try—AI can give you drafts to adjust.
- AI can shorten wandering by giving you a single clear answer instead of many scattered ones.
- Using AI for ordinary tasks builds comfort without adding pressure.

- ***If you're feeling braver today...***

Pick just one small area of your life—like home, health, or work—and ask AI, “What is one tiny way I could use you this week that would make this area feel a little lighter?” Choose only one idea it suggests and schedule a five-minute experiment with it. Ignore everything else it offers; this is about confidence, not doing more.

- “I have a jumble of thoughts about today. I am going to type them out. Can you turn them into a short, calm list of next steps?”
- “I need to write a brief note, but I am overthinking it. Here is what I want to say. Can you give me three warm, simple options?”
- “I am stuck on a small computer or document task. I will describe what I see on my screen. Can you walk me through the steps slowly?”

Chapter 7

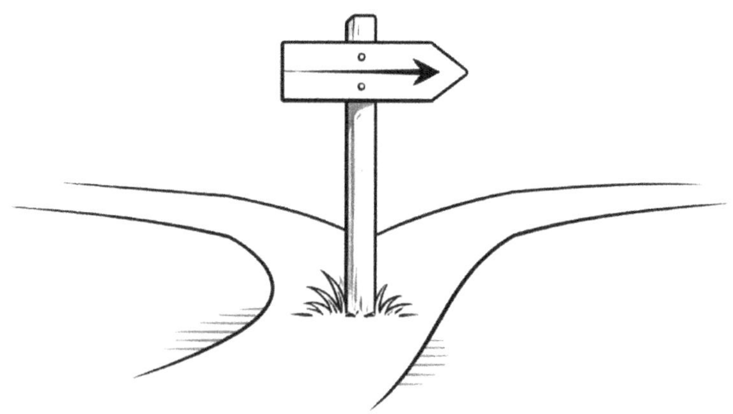

*"A gentle path with a clear horizon—
curious, but not consuming."*

Staying Curious Without Going Down Rabbit Holes

Curiosity is a wonderful thing.

It is how we learn. It is how ideas grow. It is often what brings people to AI in the first place. But curiosity without boundaries can turn into overwhelm.

If you have ever opened something "just to look" and emerged an hour later wondering where the time went, you know exactly what that feels like.

This chapter is about keeping curiosity **useful**, not exhausting.

Not Everything New Is Meant for You

One of the most valuable lessons you can learn with AI is:

You do not have to try everything just because it exists.

AI tools come with a steady stream of new features, buttons, and promises. Some are genuinely helpful. Many are just interesting. A few are distractions dressed up as solutions.

You are allowed to ignore most of them.

Curiosity does not require participation. You can be aware that something exists without feeling any obligation to use it.

Decide Your Purpose Before You Begin

Before you open AI, it helps to ask one simple question:

"What am I here for right now?"

Your answer might be:

- to think something through
- to get clarity on a specific question
- to draft or rewrite a short piece of writing
- to explore an idea briefly

When you know your purpose, it becomes much easier to stop when that purpose has been met.

Without that, it is very easy to wander.

Use AI in Short, Intentional Sessions

AI works very well in short conversations.

You do not need to stay in one long, endless session. In fact, many people get more value by:

- asking one question
- refining it once or twice
- then closing the tab or walking away

You can always come back later.

Clarity tends to “stick” better when you give it space instead of piling more information on top of the last answer.

Notice When Curiosity Turns into Noise

There is usually a moment when curiosity quietly turns into fatigue.

You might notice:

- your questions getting scattered
- answers starting to blur together
- a feeling of “too much information”
- a vague sense of restlessness or irritation

That is not a sign to push harder.

It is a sign to pause.

Stepping away does not mean you did something wrong; it means you are listening to yourself. You can simply say to AI:

"That is enough for now. Before I go, can you give me one sentence to summarize what we figured out today?"

Then close the conversation and do something offline.

Curiosity Should Feel Energizing, Not Draining

Here is a simple guideline:

- If using AI leaves you feeling clearer, lighter, or more focused—you are using it well.
- If it leaves you feeling overwhelmed or tired—it is time to stop.

There is no prize for powering through.

You are allowed to keep AI as a gentle part of your day, not an endless tunnel you fall into.

A Helpful Closing Question

One habit that can keep curiosity from turning into chaos is ending a session with:

"What is the one thing I want to remember from this?"

You can ask yourself, or you can ask AI to tell you.

That one question helps you:

- capture the value
- let go of the extra
- close the conversation on purpose

Then you can move on without feeling like there is a pile of loose ends following you.

What Comes Next

Now that you know how to stay curious without getting lost, you are ready for the next step: deciding **what to ignore, what to use, and what to wait on**.

In the next chapter, we will look at how to make calm choices about AI features and trends, so you never feel pressured to "keep up" just because the world around you is moving fast.

Takeaways

- Curiosity is good, but without boundaries it can become draining instead of helpful.
- Deciding on your purpose before you open AI makes it easier to know when to stop.
- Short, intentional sessions are often more useful than long, wandering ones.
- Noticing when you feel tired or scattered is a signal to pause, not a sign of failure.

If you're feeling braver today...

Pick one topic you are tempted to keep clicking on—something you could easily spiral about, like health, money, or news—and give it to AI with a boundary. Say, "Give me a calm, 5-sentence overview and then stop." When it answers, ask just one follow-up question to clarify what matters most for your real life, then close the tab on purpose. Treat that moment of closing as the success, not "finding every last answer."

- "Here is why I am opening you right now: [reason]. Please help me stay focused on just this, and remind me at the end what we accomplished."
- "I think I have had enough for now, but before I go, can you give me one sentence that summarizes the most important thing from this conversation?"
- "I want to use you in a short, focused way. Can you help me with this one question and then suggest a good stopping point?"

Chapter 8

"Yes, No, Later—three quiet boxes to sort the noise instead of chasing it."

What to Ignore, What to Use, and What to Wait On

One of the most helpful things you can learn about AI is not what to do.

It is what **not** to do.

When something is new and fast-moving, it is easy to feel like you are behind—especially when headlines and conversations make it sound as though everyone else is doing more, learning faster, and discovering things you somehow missed.

You have not missed anything.
You are simply choosing discernment.

What You Can Safely Ignore

Let us start with the most relieving category.

You can safely ignore:

- most "new and shiny" features
- constant updates and announcements
- tools that promise to "change everything" overnight
- advice that makes you feel rushed, afraid, or inadequate

If something feels confusing, noisy, or overly complicated, it is probably not meant for you—at least not right now.

"Not right now" is a perfectly good decision.

What Is Worth Using

The most useful parts of AI are often the simplest, and they do not change every week.

It is worth using AI to:

- ask clear, honest questions
- organize your thoughts and ideas
- clarify something you cannot quite articulate
- rewrite or refine your own words
- think through decisions calmly

These basic uses are like a solid kitchen knife or a favorite spoon: they quietly serve you repeatedly.

Once you are comfortable here, everything else becomes optional.

What Is Worth Waiting On

Some things are better explored later—or not at all.

You can wait on:

- advanced tools and plug-ins
- automation and "set it and forget it" systems

- complex setups that require multiple apps talking to each other
- anything that feels like work instead of support

You do not need to keep up with the pace of technology.

You only need to keep up with *yourself*—with what truly helps you think, decide, and live your life more peacefully.

The Myth of "Falling Behind"

A common quiet fear is:

"If I do not learn all of this now, I will be left behind."

That fear is understandable—and unnecessary.

Technology does not reward panic. It rewards thoughtful use.

When you learn at your own pace, what you learn tends to stick. When something genuinely useful shows up later, you will be in a better position to recognize it and decide calmly whether it is for you.

You have already taken the most important step: you started.

Choosing Is a Skill

Every time you decide:

- "This is helpful for me."
- "This is not for me."
- "I might look at this later."

You are building a quiet kind of confidence.

You are practicing the skill of **choosing**, instead of letting the world choose for you. That skill carries forward—not just with AI, but with other tools, invitations, and decisions in your life.

The world is full of opinions about what you *should* be doing, learning, or using. You don't need to adopt all of them. Discernment is a skill. Listening doesn't require agreement and choosing what fits you is not falling behind—it's thinking for yourself.

A Small Practice: Your "Yes / No / Later" List

To make this feel practical, you can try this exercise:

1. Think about how you have seen others talk about AI—features, tools, ideas.
2. Make three short lists on paper or in a note:
    - **Yes:** ways you already use AI or want to try.
    - **No:** things you know you are not interested in.
    - **Later:** things you might explore someday, but not now.
3. The next time you read or hear about something new, ask yourself:
    - "Does this belong on Yes, No, or Later?"

You will be surprised how quickly the noise gets quieter once you have given yourself permission to choose.

The Platform Personality Test: Which 'Thinking Partner' Fits You?

While all AI tools are built on similar "brains," they each have a slightly different "personality." Some are more academic, some are more creative, and some are more direct. Part of your **Pedagogy**, your own learning journey—is deciding which one speaks your language.

Try this experiment: Copy the exact same sentence below and paste it into two different tools (like ChatGPT and Google Gemini, or Microsoft Copilot).

The Prompt:

"I am learning how to use AI for the first time with my teacher, Fran. She says you are a 'Thinking Partner.' In three warm sentences, tell me why a person with decades of life experience is actually *better* at using AI than a teenager would be."

What to look for:

- **Tool A** might give you a bullet list of facts.
- **Tool B** might write a poetic paragraph.
- **Tool C** might sound like a professional assistant.

The Choice is Yours: There is no "best" AI. There is only one that makes you feel most comfortable. If one tool feels cold or confusing, don't blame yourself—just walk across the street and try the other "kitchen table." **You are the one who decides what fits.**

What Comes Next

Now that you know how to decide what to ignore, what to use, and what to wait on, you have a calmer foundation under your feet.

In the final chapter, we will talk about **confidence**—not technical confidence, but the kind that comes from knowing you can figure things out as you go. That is what stays with you long after the specifics of any tool change.

- You are allowed to ignore most new features, trends, and hype around AI.
- The simple, stable uses — questions, clarity, organizing, rewriting—are often the most valuable.

- "Not right now" is a valid answer when something feels too complex or noisy.
- Choosing what is for you, what is not, and what can wait builds quiet confidence.

If you're feeling braver today...

Take one thing you have heard about AI that makes you feel pressured—maybe a tool everyone is talking about, a feature you "should" learn, or a scary headline—and practice sorting it instead of reacting to it. Ask AI, "Explain this to me in calm, simple language, and then help me decide if it belongs on my Yes, No, or Later list." When you get the explanation, write down just one sentence about where it belongs for you right now, and let everything else go.

- "I am hearing about many advanced AI tools. Based on what you know of my needs, can you tell me what I can safely ignore for now?"

- "Here is how I currently use you. Can you suggest one or two simple ways to deepen that, without adding extra complexity?"
- "I do not want more noise. Can you explain which basic uses of AI will likely stay useful over time, and which things I can treat as optional experiments?"

Chapter 9

"Your choices point the way—AI is just the signpost; you are the one who decides."

Confidence Comes First — The Rest Follows

If there is one thing I hope you carry with you after this book, it is this:

You do not need to know everything to begin.
You never did.

If you have reached the point where AI feels less like a tool and more like a thinking companion, you have already learned more than you realize.

Confidence does not come from mastering every feature or keeping up with every change. It comes from realizing that you can figure things out as you go—thoughtfully, at your own pace, and without pressure.

AI does not give you confidence.
It reminds you that you already have it.

You Were Never Behind

Many people approach AI with a quiet worry that they are late to the conversation.

They are not.

Every new tool looks overwhelming until it becomes familiar. Familiarity does not come from speed. It comes from use.

You have already done the hardest part: you showed up, you asked a few questions, you stayed long enough to notice what helped and what did not.

That is more than most people ever do.

You Now Know Enough

You may not feel like an expert (you do not need to), but you now know how to:

- start a conversation without special language
- ask honest questions instead of "perfect" ones
- refine what does not feel right
- slow things down when you feel rushed
- stop when you have enough for now

That is not "beginner in the corner" behavior.
That is thoughtful use.

And it is more than enough to let AI be a real help in your daily life.

This Is a Tool, Not a Requirement

AI is not something you *have* to use.

It is something you *can* use—when it serves you.

Some days it may help you think through something small. Other days you may not open it at all. Both are fine.

The goal was never to add more noise to your life. The goal was clarity.

If AI helps you see your own thoughts more clearly, it is doing its job. If it does not, you can set it aside without apology.

Trust Yourself First

The most important relationship in all of this is not with AI.

It is with your own judgment.

If something feels helpful, keep it.
If it feels overwhelming, step away.
If it no longer fits, let it go.

That inner sense—your "this feels right for me" and "this does not"—will guide you far better than any new feature ever could.

You have been making decisions, learning new things, and adjusting to change your entire life. This is just one more place where that experience matters.

One Last Thought Before You Go

You do not need to climb the whole mountain.
You do not need to explore the entire house.
You do not need to keep up with anyone else's pace.

You just need to know that when curiosity returns—and it will—you have a place to begin.

Your shoes are already on. You know where the front door is. You have taken the first steps.

From here on, you and AI can walk together in the way that suits *you* best: calmly, honestly, and at a pace that respects the life you have already lived.

That is more than enough.

The calm, step-by-step approach I have shared here is the same one I used while helping David Selley at 87, complete his 18-book, one-year world-record publishing project as the oldest author to publish 18 books in a single year. If it can support something that ambitious, it is more than enough for your everyday questions.

Takeaways

- Confidence comes from knowing you can figure things out, not from knowing everything in advance.
- You are not late; simply starting and experimenting thoughtfully puts you ahead of most.
- AI is optional, you can use it when it serves you and ignore it when it does not.
- Your own judgment and sense of “this feels right for me” are more important than any feature.

> ***If you're feeling braver today...***
> Choose one small area of your life—home, health, work, or relationships—and ask AI, *“What’s one gentle way you could support me here this week?”* Pick just one suggestion that feels easy and doable and try it once. Notice how you feel afterward. If it helps, keep it. If not, let it go—with appreciation for the experiment.

- "Help me make a short list of what I now know how to do with you, so I can see the progress I have made."
- "Sometimes I still feel unsure about AI. Can you write a brief reminder for me that explains, in my voice, why I do not need to know everything to begin?"
- "I want to create a personal 'AI comfort plan'—how often to use you, what to use you for, and what to avoid. Can you help me outline that?"

Your Thinking Partner Toolkit

Practical prompts, easy formulas, and simple tools

— You're in Charge! —

My "No-Headache" Quick Conversation Guide

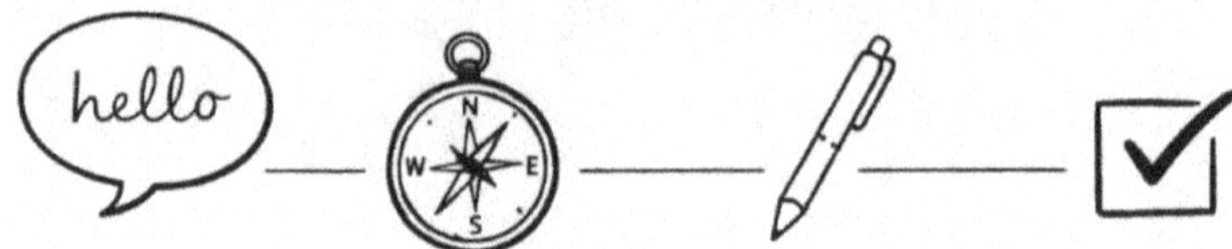

The Three-Part Formula

When you aren't sure how to ask for help, just fill in these three blanks:

1. **The Goal:** "I am trying to..."
2. **The Friction:** "...but I'm getting stuck because..."
3. **The Help:** "Can you help me [break it down / simplify this / give me 3 options]?"

Steering the Conversation

If the AI's answer doesn't feel right, use these "Steering Sentences":

- **Too much?** "That is too detailed. Give me the simple version."
- **Too stiff?** "Can you explain this as if we are at my kitchen table?"

- **Not what you meant?** "That’s not quite it. Let’s try again, focusing on..."
- **Unsure?** "Why did you suggest that approach?"

The "Stay Calm" Reminders

- **Vague In = Vague Out.** This isn't failure; it's just feedback.
- **Talk in Sentences.** AI prefers a conversation over a list of commands.
- **Stop When You’re Full.** If you feel scattered or tired, close the tab.
- **You Are the Boss.** AI is the assistant; you have the life experience.

"For Thinking Deeper"

Safe Places to Start

• **The Rebuttal:** “You suggested I try [Idea]. Can you tell me two or three reasons why this might not be a good fit for someone who values [Your Value, e.g., a quiet morning]?”
• **The Blind Spot:** “What is one potential drawback

or 'catch' to this plan that I might be missing because I am focused on the positive side?"

- **The "Peace of Mind" Check:** "If I choose to ignore this advice, what is the most likely consequence? Help me weigh the pros and cons side-by-side."
- **The Alternative Path:** "I'm not sure I agree with your reasoning. Can you give me a completely different perspective that challenges what you just told me?"
- **The Reasoning Routine:** "I'm feeling a bit overwhelmed by this. Let's look at this slowly and find the 'why nots' before I decide what to do."

My AI Breakthroughs & Notes

Use this space to capture the moments when the "tech headache" faded and clarity took its place.

The "Aha!" Moments

Jot down a time AI surprised you, helped you get unstuck, or made a heavy task feel light.

- **Date: ________ What happened:**

  ____

- **Date: ________ What happened:**

  ____

My Favorite "Steering" Sentences

Which phrases felt most like "you" when you were guiding the conversation?

- ____
- ____
- ____
- ____

My "Yes" List

What are the 2 or 3 small things you've decided are truly worth using AI for?

1. ____
2. ____
3. ____

Moments of Discernment

Write down a time you chose to stop, walk away, or ignore the "noise" because you had enough.

____

A Final Reminder: "You do not need to climb the whole mountain... Your shoes are already on."

My "No Headache" AI Checklist

It's All About the Questions

These are the habits I lean on myself—simple, repeatable, and kind.

1. Start with a "hello."

You do not need the perfect question; you just need to begin. One honest sentence is enough.

2. Say what you're here for.

Begin with one line of purpose: "I'm here to get clarity on...", "I just need help with...".

3. Ask in sentences, not commands.

"Can you help me..." works better than single words like "Summarize" or "Rewrite."

4. Give a little context.

Add one line about you: "I'm new to this," "I tend to overthink," "I want a warm tone."

5. Treat confusion as feedback, not failure.

If an answer feels off, say, "That's not quite what I meant. Let me explain it differently."

6. Use AI to think, not just to hurry.
Ask it to walk through things with you: "Help me think this through step by step."

7. Keep sessions short and intentional.
One question, one refinement, then pause. You can always come back later.

8. Stop when you feel full.
If you feel tired or scattered, that is your signal to close the tab, not to push harder.

9. Protect your private details.

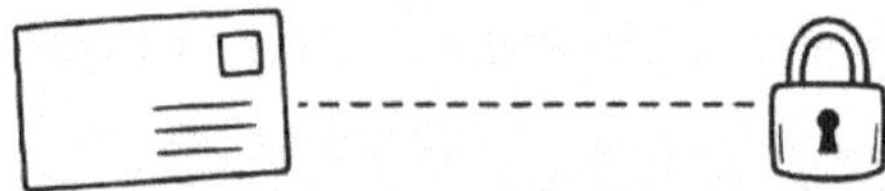

Never share passwords, bank numbers, or anything you would not write on a postcard.

10. Remember who is in charge.
AI is the assistant. You are the one with the life experience. You always get the final say.

My Favorite First Step Prompts

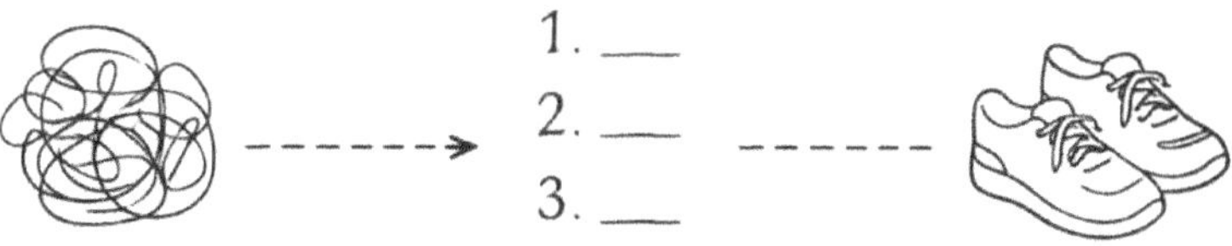

More Prompts!

You do not need to sound clever. You can copy these exactly and change just a few words.

For clarity and calm

- "I feel scattered today. I'm going to tell you what's on my mind. Can you turn it into a short, calm to-do list with no more than five items?"
- "I'm not sure what my real question is yet. Can you ask me a few gentle questions to help me find it?"

For everyday tasks

- "I need to write a short note, but I'm overthinking it. Here's what I want to say in my own messy words. Can you give me three simple versions that sound warm and natural?"

- “I’m stuck on a small computer/document task. I’ll describe what I see. Can you walk me through the steps slowly and clearly?”

For learning without overwhelm

- “I keep hearing about [topic]. I’m new to this. Can you explain it in plain language, in under 200 words?”
- “Give me a very simple overview of [topic], then three questions I could ask you next if I want to understand more.”

For memories and legacy

- “I want to capture a memory about [event/person]. Can you ask me five questions to help me remember the details?”
- “Here are some scattered notes about my life story. Can you group them into possible chapter themes?”

For decisions

- “I’m deciding between a few options. I’ll describe them. Can you list the pros and cons for each, and then one gentle next step for me?"

Use these as training wheels. You will soon start writing your own versions without thinking about it.

The Human at the Center

In a world filled with apps and programs promising to "optimize" your life or make you "better," this series takes a different path. We are not here to turn you into a machine or to follow a rigid software script.

AI is the assistant; you are the boss.

The **AI for Everyday Life Series** is built on the belief that technology is simply a new way for the human heart to say "hello" to the future. My **Pedagogy** is designed to honor the decades of wisdom, curiosity, and experience you already carry.

While other tools might offer a shortcut, we are interested in **clarity**. We use AI as a patient **Thinking Partner** to:

- **Refine your own unique voice**, not replace it.

- **Untangle messy thoughts** at your own kitchen table.
- **Restore your confidence** in the way you've always made sense of things.

You don't need a complicated program to "fix" you. You simply need a gentle way to rediscover the power of your own thinking.

How This Book Was Created (AI-Assisted, Human-Led)

You'll notice I talk about AI like a thinking partner, because that's exactly how I used it while shaping this book.

I wrote the ideas, stories, teaching philosophy, and guidance from my own experience. I used AI to help me organize sections, test clarity, tighten wording, and explore better ways to explain beginner concepts—similar to how a writer might use an editor, a coach, or a brainstorming partner.

I did not use AI to replace my judgment. I used it to support my thinking.

Technology changes fast, but human discernment doesn't. That's the heart of this book—and the heart of this series.

Promptings Publishing was born from a simple desire: to help ordinary people turn their hard-won wisdom into something they can hold in their hands and share.

After more than fifty years working with words — beginning with my first business, a graphics and typesetting studio in Hollywood in 1971 — and moving through more entrepreneurial adventures than I can count, I found myself drawn back to what I have always loved most: shaping ideas into something tangible.

Out of my own projects, pivots, and persistence, this work evolved naturally.

I understand what it feels like to carry experience, lessons, and insight — and not quite know how to turn them into a book.

Today, I help entrepreneurs and everyday experts do exactly that, with clarity, structure, and deep respect for their voice.

Promptings Publishing exists to bridge that gap.

I specialize in working with:

- People who feel overwhelmed by the idea of writing a book.
- Beginners who don't feel technical.
- Heart-centered entrepreneurs who want a thoughtful, human book instead of a rushed product.

How We Work Together The same step-by-step approach you experienced in this book is the one I use with my authors: calm, clear, and kind. Together, we use a mix of gentle conversation, clear structure, and simple AI tools to take messy drafts and turn them into readable chapters, while shaping a book's flow and voice so it sounds like *you*.

Classes, Events, and 1-on-1 Coaching

If you aren't ready for a full publishing project but want to learn the ropes, I also offer:

- **"How to Publish Your Own Book" Events:** Gentle workshops that demystify the path from a blank page to a finished book.
- **AI for Beginners Classes:** Hands-on sessions where we practice using AI as your patient "Thinking Partner" for your specific writing projects.
- **Author Series Workshops:** Group events focused on the different topics in the *AI for Everyday Life* series.

Personalized 1-on-1 Coaching For those who want a dedicated guide, I offer private, 1-on-1 coaching sessions. I will walk with you through the entire process, teaching you how to:

- **Write and Format**: Use AI to help organize your thoughts and prepare your manuscript so it looks professional.
- **Publish on Amazon**: Navigate the "tech headaches" of the Amazon platform so your book is available for the world to see.
- **Find Your Voice**: Ensure the final product sounds like you, keeping your heart at the center of the story.

I specialize in helping beginners who ‘don’t feel technical’ turn messy drafts into readable chapters. If you have a book, story, or legacy project ‘in the hopper,’ I would love to hear about it.

Visit www.PromptingsPublishing.com

or email me at franjessee@gmail.com

An Invitation to

BUSINESS WITH PURPOSE

PUBLISHING

I am proud to be a founding member and the publishing partner for Business With Purpose, a nonprofit community of heart-centered entrepreneurs, creators, and guides who believe business can be a force for good.

Business With Purpose operates under the nonprofit leadership of co-founders Cherri Pedrioli and Sue Brooke, whose commitment to purpose-driven education anchors the organization. The original vision for the Built With Purpose movement was sparked by Sue Brooke, whose idea continues to grow through collaboration and shared service.

Together, Sue and I are building the *Built With Purpose* compilation book series—projects that bring real stories from real entrepreneurs into beautifully crafted books that reflect heart, clarity, and credibility.

In a noisy world, Business With Purpose focuses on:

- meaningful connections instead of empty networking
- collaboration instead of competition
- education that feels human, not high-pressure

My role includes:

- serving as publisher for our book projects
- guiding authors through the compilation and Expert Series process
- helping beginners feel safe using AI as a thinking partner
- adding warmth and clarity to the words our members use to share their stories

If this book has helped you feel a little less intimidated and a little more curious, you are exactly the kind of person we love to welcome—whether you are self-employed, just exploring, or simply looking for a community that values purpose over noise.

You do not have to figure out your next chapter alone.

Please visit

www.BusinessWithPurpose.org

About the Author

Fran Jessee —

From Typesetting to AI for Everyday Life

Fran Jessee is an entrepreneur, publisher, and gentle guide for beginners who feel intimidated by technology, writing, or “putting themselves out there.”

Her journey began in 1971 with Fran Jessee Typesetting in Hollywood, where she built a thriving typesetting shop serving designers and printers in the recording and entertainment industries. Over the decades, she went on to create and run multiple ventures—including a successful Etsy invitation shop and Longevity Spice Blends, where she became known as “Fran the Spice Lady” for her health-focused spice blends and teaching.

Today, Fran channels more than fifty years of creative and business experience into Promptings Publishing, where she helps authors and beginners turn their ideas into finished books without the usual tech headaches.

In 2025, she served as the publisher and project “engineer” for author David Selley’s 18-book, one-year world-record publishing project, in which he became the oldest author to publish 18+1 books in a single year. Fran used the same calm, conversational AI methods you have seen in this book to organize material, clarify structure, and keep the project moving forward. AI was used as a thinking partner. The ideas, stories, tone, and voice are authentically his.

Alongside her publishing work, Fran is a founding member of Business With Purpose, where she teaches “simple and easy AI for everyday life” and supports entrepreneurs in expressing their vision and story in clear, human language.

Her work—whether with spices, stories, or AI—has always centered around one quiet gift: making hard things feel simple and helping people who feel overwhelmed remember that they are not behind and not alone.

The AI for Everyday Life Series

This book is part of the **AI for Everyday Life** series—a collection of short, approachable guides designed to help real people use AI calmly, confidently, and without overwhelm. Each book in the series focuses on one simple question, so you can start where you are and explore only what matters to you.

"If you find yourself curious about using AI for other parts of life—decisions, writing, food, health—this book is part of a small, growing series you can explore when and if it feels useful".

FIRST RELEASE

AI for Beginners

No Tech Headaches Required

How to Use AI as a Thinking Partner — Not a Shortcut

A gentle, human introduction to AI that shows you how to begin — without jargon, judgment, or stress.

AI for Beginners is part of the **FOUNDATIONS, HELPERS, AND LIFE SITUATIONS SERIES** continued the following pages.

See the following pages for additional AI learning subjects to be released soon!

FOUNDATIONS

AI for Writing

Let's Get It Out of Your Head and Onto the Page

A supportive guide for turning thoughts into words while keeping your voice, clarity, and confidence intact.

AI for Clarity

How to Think Clearly in a Noisy World
Losing Your Mind or Your Judgment

AI for Clarity is for thoughtful people who want to remain steady and fully in charge in a noisy world.

AI for Fun

Playful Ways to Explore Your World—Just Because

Playful, curiosity-driven ways to explore ideas, interests, and creativity with no agenda attached.

HELPERS

AI for Health

The Energy Door I Didn't Know Existed

How I Used AI as a Thinking Partner to Make Sense of Food, Health, and the Energy I Was Searching For.

AI for Food

Finding the Energy I Was Looking For

Turning Food into Energy — Fuel for Your Body: Using AI to ask the right questions about Food, Nutrition, and the Patterns That Shape You.

HELP! My Computer isn't Working

A calm, practical guide to handling tech problems people usually call tech support for showing you how to use AI to understand what's wrong, ask right questions, and fix everyday computer issues step by step without panic.

AI for The Nest

Keeping Life, Family, and Home Without Losing Yourself

Organizing the Chaos of Everyday Living A guide to using AI as a quiet household assistant to manage schedules and home logistics, turning your space back into a sanctuary.

AI for Finances

Making Sense of Numbers Without the Headache

A gentle approach to budgets and financial terms, helping you look at your numbers clearly to find a simple path toward peace.

AI for Adventure

Finding the Joy in the Journey

Clearing the logistics headache of travel and hobbies so you can focus on the experience and the joy of discovery.

LIFE SITUATIONS

AI for Decisions

When You're Stuck and Can't Land Anywhere

When everything feels uncertain this helps you untangle your thinking and step forward with confidence.

AI for Overwhelm

When Everything Feels Like Too Much

Explore how AI can help you untangle mental clutter and regain a sense of steadiness when small things feel heavy.

AI for Transitions

Thinking Through Change Without Losing Yourself.

f

A thoughtful companion for retirement, loss, or reinvention that supports reflection while you move through change at your own pace.

AI for Conversation

Finding the Right Words Without Overthinking

Help for difficult topics and moments when tone matters, showing you how to practice what you want to say while keeping your voice natural.

AI for Legacy

Preserving what matters one question at a time.

Using AI as a patient interviewer to help you record memories and life lessons, turning messy thoughts into stories for the next generation.

THE CAPSTONE

AI for For Minds Like Mine

Making Sense of How You Make Sense

A supportive guide for thinkers who loop, analyze, and revisit—helping you organize thoughts, calm mental noise, and work *with* your brain instead of against it.

A Final Note

• These books were written for people who want AI to feel supportive, not intimidating.

• You don't need to be technical.

• You don't need to rush.

• You don't need to know everything.

• You don't need to use AI as a shortcut.

Instead, you can use it as a thinking partner.

A place to lay out your thoughts.

A place to slow down.

A place to ask better questions.

A place to think things through before reacting.

AI works best not when it replaces your thinking — but when it strengthens it.

www.ingramcontent.com/pod-product-compliance
Lightning Source LLC
LaVergne TN
LVHW010925110826
845149LV00013B/2478